TWO MINDS

TWO MINDS

Poems

Callie Siskel

W. W. NORTON & COMPANY
Independent Publishers Since 1923

For information about permission to reproduce selections from this book,
write to Permissions, W. W. Norton & Company, Inc., 500 Fifth Avenue,
New York, NY 10110

For information about special discounts for bulk purchases, please contact
W. W. Norton Special Sales at specialsales@wwnorton.com or 800-233-4830

Manufacturing by Versa Press
Production manager: Julia Druskin

ISBN 978-1-324-07367-3

W. W. Norton & Company, Inc., 500 Fifth Avenue, New York, N.Y. 10110
www.wwnorton.com

W. W. Norton & Company Ltd., 15 Carlisle Street, London W1D 3BS

1 2 3 4 5 6 7 8 9 0

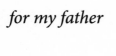

for my father

Contents

TWO MINDS

I am waiting behind the house among the ash trees

Twenty-three winters have passed

without interruption

Under the frozen grass, the same earth

Nearby a woodpecker drills into the tree's dead cells

Bark on top of heartwood on top of pith

Over and over the bird braces for impact

its body built to endure such blows

So loud I barely notice two squirrels warring

between the pickets

I have seen many living things mark their territory

where I am standing—

The seasons remove their traces, in spite of us all

Mise en Abyme

I was a lot to carry in summer.
High winds shook the round windows
for which the hospital is known.
It was a Saturday, midday; I was upside-down.
They cut her open to lift me out.
The swaddle and hat were too small,
so I was wrapped inside a towel.
My name pleased both sides of the family—
a shared consonance with my mother's father,
an overall sound with my father's mother.
I came home to a sister who thought I belonged
to someone else. "Marie," she said to the nurse,
"You forgot your baby."
Somewhere on earth is my Matryoshka doll.
Rarely did I open her: I preferred to hear
her wooden offspring knocking around inside—
the son with the broom and the daughter
with a scythe. The baby in the patchwork quilt,
I pitied—it would never hold anything.
My grandmother, the youngest of her siblings,
fled Russia as a child and brought nothing with her.
She remembers her bedroom being black.
She never carried my father,
she adopted him from her sister (who died
hiding her cancer, the way my father did).
No generation lives neatly inside another.

To play with the doll was to disassemble her.
When I did, I closed each one so that the head
was misaligned, the seam exposed,
the flowers on the matron's dress discontinuous.
When I returned them to her, I'd leave one doll
out completely, wondering what it would be like
to live outside of one's family.
Maybe before there were lips, there was already a whisper
And leaves circled around in treelessness . . .
Maybe before we were born, we existed,
Mandelstam is saying.
That day in July, closer to the end of a century
than the middle, would have gone on the same
without me—high wind, high heat.

Fugue

We checked each room for our parents.
Kate checked their bedroom. I checked the den.
Our mother had been reading—her book open
and face down on her favorite chair.
In the living room, someone had set out music,
the pages futile against the piano.
I ran to the window. Kate, to the door.
You were not born yet.
I could hear the warning from the park—
a recording that played all night:
Stay off the ice.
The ice is thin.
There were human faces on a television
in the apartment across the street.
A whir that could have been cars in the far distance
or the wind wrapping around the buildings
or snow falling from the eaves
resounded through the glass.
After all, you were not born yet.
Then our parents came down the hallway
in their robes, having been asleep the entire time.
When they called to us,
I stayed where I was. I wanted to see them
without me too.

Invitation

My initials curled inside the oval like three robins
crowding a tree hollow.

The cardstock was beveled, the envelopes lined in airy pink paper.

My father was dying

quietly like the sound of his pen lifting
then touching down again.

Once, waking from a nap, he asked me, "Will I be okay?"
and I said, "Yes."

Then it was time to chant Torah. I'd been called to fill the
    sanctuary
by a new Hebrew name, a derivative of "life."

I liked it—the chance to be divested of particulars, to be marked
    instead
by the narrative of crossing, which was my Torah portion, Exodus,

Moses stretching out his hand over the sea and then God parting it
    in half

like a child's hair,

and the Israelites walking into the midst upon dry ground
like the ground I was standing on,

January, a freshly shoveled street on which the thinnest layer of snow
covers the cement, then turns back into water.

Succession

I heard by phone.
I woke up to what I had slept through.
Rain pelting my friend's car window.
I was not there, but my mother was—
she is always there at the end.
Afterward, I walked in on her
sitting on my grandmother's bed,
the quilt green with white irises,
calling my sister, consoling the air.
We went home.
I found my baby brother.
I tried to say it with my eyes.
He was running with a balloon down the hallway.
In a hurry.
My father wrote us a goodbye letter
that we were handed much later,
the script so tight, I can barely read it.
He'd wanted to tell us himself.
The weight of it: three sheets.

Bird in Space

In New York, no one could believe it was art, it left too much to the imagination.

Under a skylight, I circled it—wingless, polished, unattended—as if I were its bride.

I regarded a nearby landscape whose perspective was clear: man's dominion over nature.

I wanted to touch the bird, so I knew it was art, not by how it appeared but by what it elicited.

Did I want to be the artist or the bird that will not explain itself?

There is freedom in that.

A couple walked past me on their way to the contemporary wing, using a map to guide them toward the bright and unmistakable colors.

The light had shifted, the gallery now empty, a shadow fell evenly across its breast, which was also its nape and belly and flank.

Husband and Wife

There's two of them! They're floating
toward each other, my mother said,
backing away from where the pool was brimming
over the pavement, where she'd wanted to sit
and wet her feet. I couldn't see them
from where I stood, just my mother pacing
slowly, which felt familiar. Watching her, I knew
they weren't the bees from lunch, which were likely
a single bee reappearing over the fruit, then circling
our empty cans. To her, they were lovers.
They were trying to reach each other. All my life,
I've watched her make couples out of everything—
even the napkin rings. She waited until the bees
had met before she cupped them in her hands.

Marrying Houses

Some women marry houses.
—ANNE SEXTON

My mother's first husband was my father;
her second husband was her house.
She wasn't wedded to one in particular.
She transferred her love

each time we moved, calling them all *home*,
surprising them with flowers, monthly
memberships to individually wrapped fruit.
When the house had a woman's needs,

she was also its husband. The kitchen
was the bedroom, so to speak. It required
the most care. That's where, at sunrise,
they could be alone. I would wake

to what love looked like and smelled like:
polished brass, vinegar on wood.
She'd use her hand to crease each pillow.
Even our sink so clean

I could see my reflection in it.
Now I can picture our houses more clearly
than my father, who often fell asleep
in rooms we weren't allowed to go into.

I think she wanted to show me houses
could be a husband, only more lasting.
Like a mortician, she made them
more beautiful than they were in life.

Cocktail Hour

On nights my mother's boyfriend
    stayed over, I would come home
from school and find his Reeboks
       straightened on the welcome mat.

The interior door would be open—
    the house alive with the Allman Brothers'
"Ramblin' Man" or "Midnight Rider,"
       and every light would be on

except inside the bathrooms,
    where she'd lit candles, sending
the smell of gardenias burning
       toward the bedroom hall. I'd shrug

my bag off in my room and walk toward
    the kitchen—find a pot percolating
with meat sauce, a wooden spoon, half-soaked
       in orange liquid, resting on the lid.

On the counter: a bottle of wine chilling
    inside a bucket of ice, a stack
of square napkins, a block of cheese,
       cured meat, a saucer of olive oil,

into which someone had already dipped
    bread. I'd know where they were,
taking their time, drinking clear
        cocktails in the living room.

There, I'd announce myself, tall, indignant
    as a man, inside the doorway—
as if I were my father, coming home
        early, hungry for dinner.

Overwinter

January—which only yesterday
I learned means doors

One winter he came into
the world; another, he left

The doors seem closer now,
wide as winter, hinged with snow

Such a soft way to be merciless—

January, presiding over birth
and death as if it weren't a conflict
of interest, as paradoxical

and purposeful as Jacob
digging his own grave   Hand over fist

my father's final days
slipped through my fingers

Hard to hold something
whose fit in your hand

is accidental

Birds sheer south

See how they do not look back
I am like you, January

I hear the sound
of the brass knob rolling in the cold
of his hand,
watch the light lengthen

on the floor   Yes he was here
I heard you say *Come in, come in*

Messenger

Picture a symbol of what you want
to remember. An anchor for the sea,

a cuirass for a battle scene.
I see my mother's knife, the one

she used to open her mail.
Its dull blade—the sheer force

of it splitting the seal.
The antiquated sheath that held

its tongue. It was her tongue that cut
my childhood in half.

Her mouth that had to say
exactly what I cannot remember,

but which, if I could repeat, might
somehow un-divide me.

Echo

In the long hallway, everyone's doors were closed.

I touched every doorknob and saw myself magnified.

When I was let into a room, I sat at the end of the bed—

I refused to sleep in my own.

I put my hands inside slippers and crawled around.

I was a child—

a jealous woman made me.

When she said, "My pain is greater than your pain,"

I said, "Your pain."

That I should originate anything

was intolerable to me,

but I considered it, privately.

To echo is not to repeat, but to diminish.

Winter turned to spring, and I watched everyone

grow bigger in my absence.

Caravaggio's *Narcissus*

The surface of the water
does not offer perspective,
only the flat reality of the boy
in a puffed-up jacket,
crouched over water so darkly lit
one might mistake it
for high gloss on a stained floor.

No, that's the earth
under his hands, one hand at the water's edge,
the other, turned inward, immersed.
A single knee exposed—
the moon lost in its orbit
around a void.
The water unites
the boy and what the boy sees.
The water is the means; it does not *mean* anything.
Who would want to tell the boy
his knee is not the moon?

I want to tell the boy, *keep looking*,
brush the hair from his eye,
rotate his hand so his wrist
does not tire,
free his calf from the weight
of his knee.

Mostly, I want to be water,
the source of his love.

But I am on the ground
re-creating the painting
looking down at my rug—
one hand on the fringe,
the other on the wood floor,
my knee already in pain
my heel sharp against my groin.

But at what cost?
I pay someone to ask me again and again and again.

June Gloom

It is gray and viscous, and I'm waiting for it to burn off.
My sister was just here visiting. I brought her her tea,

folded towels. I said many things silently to myself like
bamboo training Phalaenopsis, shaping and protecting it, but

also reining it back. She was disappointed in the weather,
that we agreed on. That, and how we would have made

different choices in life if we could. (But we could.)
We fill days this way, peeling carrots, watching the ribbons

of weathered skin make loose shapes on the board. When
I sweep up the scraps, I am reminded of a phrase I wrote

down on the back of a fabric sample: *Everything activates
loss.* I don't want something that obvious to be true. I have

been searching for a good thesis. I look up "stuck" and
find "related to German *sticken, embroider,*" which makes

me feel better. I might be in the middle of a necessary
stitch. In an ad on Instagram, a yellow bra promises

"Brighter Days Ahead," or is it citrine? It is something a
version of me once wanted and the algorithm, comfortingly,

can't keep up. I am too bitter now for lace. The fabric sample was called Coastal Linen in Platinum. There was

also Eco Weave in Oyster, Slub Cotton in Stone, Textured Twill in Light Gray, Brushed Crossweave in Natural,

Washed Linen Cotton in Silver Taupe, and Heathered Basketweave in Dove. It took me two years to decide.

On my desk, the bouquet I bought for her arrival: roses, lilies, carnations, and chrysanthemums. I will miss early

summer, how the murmurings of impending heat remind me of human fragility. It will likely be the hottest summer

on record, because that's how it goes. The record keeps expanding. One day it should say, no, I won't hold that

for you. I could say the same thing to my sister. Or to myself. I could and I don't, and I see that more now that

the sky is like Basketweave Dove, matte and unreflective. What would that feel like? To say something in real time.

Transparent Man

The garment bag was black like any other,
but through the plastic window I could see

a square of white fabric. Before I saw
Saturday Night Fever, that's how I knew

the polyester suit, whose wide lapels
opened onto a slick-black shirt, sewn deep

into the pants. I would have never pictured
bell-bottoms on a man, but there they were

on Tony Manero (John Travolta),
staring into an iridescent light,

pointing his right index finger toward
the ceiling as the dance floor changed colors.

My father saw the movie seventeen times,
and bought that suit, the exact one, at auction.

I asked my mother why he kept it shut
in cedar, hanging on a rack with all

our winter coats, and not inside his closet,
where, later, I buried my face inside

his jackets. Why didn't we display it?
That's not who he was, my mother said.

Besides, it almost stood up by itself.
It had to, no one ever tried it on.

Once, I opened the garment bag and peered
inside to see a different actor, one

who seemed to play my father, full of light,
a young, transparent man dressed up in white.

Mourner's Logic

When the congregation assembles,
I look to the chorus, modeling
wholeness, how to remain intact.
Absorbed in music,
its supplications, they seem purer,
don't they? Those whose voices
make meaning, while their bodies
dematerialize, or mean to, or should.
They sing *Avinu Malkeinu, Our Father,
Our King*. One in a blue cardigan
with a brooch—I find myself drawn
to her in particular. *Whole*
comes from *hail*: to attract attention.
I choose her as one might elevate
a tulip from a bowl, relocating it

to its own vase. Watch
as I hand her this awful gift
of recognition, as if I fastened
her brooch or made her up
entirely. As mourners, we rise
when the names of those
we have lost are called.
And when I was a child,

I thought *God chose me for this.*
Is death a sword that knights
the living? I kind of believe it is.

Jeanne

My boss told me I look like a Modigliani.
He wasn't the only one.

A young woman's face, long and plaintive, or
sadder than plaintive—moribund.

Her head on her neck like a leaf on a pear.
The eyes uneven.

Nearly every woman he painted was his wife,
Jeanne Hébuterne. Jeanne on her side.

In a wide-brim hat. Jeanne in a bistro chair
with her hands on her lap or touching her throat.

On my psychology textbook in college,
I saw her from the shoulders up—

her neck, exalted, her mouth a crumb,
the chin tilted down as if to say,

"I'm yours."
She's the perfect cover for a book

that tries to explain how the mind develops
and how it breaks down.

The day after her husband died,
she leapt from a window.

She was pregnant.
She had a daughter named Jeanne.

She looked nothing like the paintings.
Her face was round, her lips full.

She did lower her chin
at least in photographs.

When told I look like a man's image
of a woman, I believe it.

I do not. Nor do I look like Jeanne,
who left behind four paintings of her own:

Two still lifes, a portrait of her husband,
and a portrait of herself.

Prophecy in Blue

When I open the book, the poet
becomes her own prophet:

the established blue of heaven
appears on the page where one

blue thread reveals itself
inside the binding. This has to be

the only place where we see
what's holding it together.

My prediction comes true,
as if the word *blue* produced

the thread, a printer's mistake.
In the poem, we're left bending

before a grave. I begin to see
the thread as a figure for grief.

Why this need to eke out meaning
from every errant thing?

We're holding on to something—
the blue thread binding us

to one persistent memory,
my father in synagogue, praying

for himself inside his navy suit.

Heir

See the I asking to join her?
Once, I thought Grief

could have two heirs—
two crowns of daisies, two coronations

in a field of bitterweed.
Two shadows bleating

one prayer. Mother and daughter's
faces receding

in one mirror,
but one was chosen,

arranged the hierarchy,
the silverware, the fork

on its own, while I, unaware
that Grief does not divide

evenly, shuttled a yolk
between two shells

until it broke. The fantasy.
Of fruit with no pit.

Of us both in the room
where he died, windows

on all sides. Grief bequeaths
the I, each wanting a stage,

a soliloquy, even I long
to be the plaintive one now.

Narcissus

Time's Person of the Year was "You."

I was a sophomore in college. I held the mirror up to my friend.

Outside a fraternity, I stood in a circle of women telling each other
how pretty they were.

On the walk back to my room, I passed a monument: water running
over granite.

The man I loved wanted me in his bed, so I could tell him he was
exceptional.

There is a difference between Echo and the spring: one repeats, one
colludes.

In his childhood bed, we had sex, and I turned bright red.

He said, "Someone had a good time," and I knew it was over.

I moved out of the dorm with my friend, paid less for the smaller
room.

At dinner, she said the chef was staring at her. I agreed.

If I told you how she stranded me, the focus would shift to her, as it
   always did.

There is beauty in submission, but it depends on what one gains from it.

When a poet came to campus, old and failing, she bared herself like a
   wet stone drying.

Paean

The peonies never bloomed.
One opened slightly, if that counts,
the others deepened in color.
I kept trimming them below the leaves
under the sink,
the way my mother taught me
and was taught by her mother.
(Once, in front of her,
she said, "If I get like that,
lead me deep into the forest
and then turn around."
"I would never do that," I said.
"Then I will ask your sister," she said.)
I thought to call her for help,
but the water was acrid,
and the buds, firm to the touch
a week ago, felt hollow.
I will open them by hand,
I thought, but there were no
discernable petals.
After I threw them away,
I swept up the breakable leaves
that had fallen to the floor,
I poured the water from the vase
in the shape of a woman's head,
the eyebrows arched.

Where the peonies had been
there was now an opening—
the mind waiting to be filled again.

George Clausen's *Youth Mourning*

A naked girl
in the fetal position

faces a cross
in dry grass.

Beyond her, craters
full of water.

Beyond that,
the sea.

The painter, her father,
must have seen her

pre-widowed and pristine
like an unturned stone,

her hands shielding
her head,

her breast
against her knee.

This is mourning—
so poised,

she already knows
what the war

will ask of her.
Tell me her body

will do more
than decorate the field.

The Plans

When my parents stood beside
    the broken ground, our future
        was already written in the soil,

where the grass had snapped
        at the stem. That's when our house
            was still a blueprint,

a nameless constellation,
    flapping in the breeze, and the views
        from all rooms seemed vast, windowless.

Halfway up the mound, our car
        was parked on a makeshift driveway,
            a steep ascent above a dead-end beach,

a band of yellow and motionless
    green, blocked by a fuse box, circuiting
        nothing. I watched him from the street—

he was laying down stones to stake out
    the boundaries. Then he called my name,
        held me up and out toward the house

next door. An ice-blue pool rippled
    in bleached concrete. *This is the view*
        from your room. If a plan was a promise

to me then, our lot was a burial ground,
    the future site of a pine-planked frame,
        a house new owners would slowly fill in,

adding siding and a gray fence,
    cutting off the access we had left,
        apart from the plans, which we kept.

Mirror Image

When he was alive, we rode the elevator.
I recall his reflection in the brass doors

more easily than his body next to mine.
Absence is not absolute; it's insidious.

It leaves us the mirror image. My face,
for example. My brother's. His stance.

Aubade

Sometimes, before school, my mother would pin a note to me, too close to my chin to read, folded horizontally. I'd look down at the pin, which had been in her mouth, never asking what she wrote to whom.

It seemed related to my growing doubt that she would be there when I came home, and when she was, she looked like a paper cutout, her back to me, in front of the window with the park outside, the lake beyond.

I rummaged through her drawers, read her letters. On our old phone, I would pick up the receiver slowly enough to deaden the hook switch —listen to her voice, unmediated by motherhood like her face unmade before bed.

I had thought she was going to leave with my father, the two of them so in love I felt unnecessary. When we traveled as a family, she would tell me and my sister to walk ahead.

If she read this now, she'd say, "Is that all you remember?"

No. She dressed us and packed lunches and styled our hair with the wide tooth comb that came to a point. She held it in her mouth against her teeth, while she used her hands to tie our braids like an animal who gives her whole body to her young. She did that, and she wrote me letters as the Tooth Fairy about the long trip she had made to arrive at my room, and how she was tempted to wake me and tell me she liked my chin.

But she didn't wake me. I never felt her hand under my pillow or saw her feet breaking the seam of light under the door.

Women in Portraiture

I think about women in portraiture
known for the thing they hold.

And for you, this cape,
Titian could have said, exposing

her right shoulder, separating her
from Girl with a Platter of Fruit.

With Fan. In Furs. In a Black Robe
with a Globe and Compass.

But naked Venus of Urbino
has one hand around some roses

and the other on herself,
the fingers curled

inward, listless, grazing.
And if she let go?

Emissary

In college, I learned the phrase *form and function*. I fell in love with my professor from a distance. I changed my "world view." When sun through cantilevered windows illuminated *lux et veritas* on a stone frontispiece, I realized truth is an equinox, an instance of overlaying. I went to college where my father did. A legacy, as in "a person delegated," sent by someone else. Rumor had it that he once climbed the clocktower dressed as Batman. I would look up at midnight and see a familiar silhouette obscuring the clock face. When he was sick, I stared into his marbled green alarm clock, the color of lake water, lightening as we waded through it, our knees glowing orange in the long afternoon. We were headed to the sandbar, also known as *shoal*, just shy of shore. I felt him there in college, but I never told anyone. I heard his voice in the katydids from my dorm, announcing when summer, carried over, had morphed into fall. If I were speaking to myself in that echo chamber it would not have changed much, not the feeling

that my father had slept in the same place
exactly forty years before. In my room, I
imagined him thinking about every good
thing coming: the newspaper, the city,
the 70s, his mother's pride. *Foreshadow,
adumbrate, portend*: I applied these words
to my books until everything coalesced.
Everything happens for a reason is the logic
of remembering. Those clocks. That lake.
In the library, I tracked down the books
of his mentor, thinking what if he held
what I am holding now.

Giverny

There is nothing in the garden
as yellow as the dining room.
Nothing as opaque.

A single buttery shade
covers the walls and closes
around the furniture.

Two lengths of rope
tie off the room from Monet's house
as though warning of wet paint.

It's lacquer and sunlight
through the patio doors that gives
the illusion of liquid

where there is none,
where everything is set.
Even the yellow table,

draped in white
and the eight cane-back chairs,
each one pushed in

to a willowware plate
and a crystal glass
we couldn't raise.

You were my father
for nearly thirteen years.
I asked you why

we weren't allowed
to touch anything that day.
Who knew

the room would go unchanged?
That we would be outlasted
by a heavy coat of paint.

Diegesis

The neighbors across from me have one boy and one girl. I hear the slow notes of their piano while I'm reading— the father, a musician, must be teaching them. They respond improvidently with strong, uneven glissandos like a sound bridge in a film signaling discordance.

Their yard runs along the longest side of my apartment where all of my windows are. A row of cypresses lines the driveway between us but goes only halfway. I can look down and see the daughter kicking a ball at the chain-link fence, singing to herself, intermittently. The son is a mystery. Often, I cross paths with the mother standing at the iron gate, waving off the children or waving them back in. Sometimes we lock eyes, and I want to go inside with her as the daughter

asking to be fed. In a story, one might call this rising action; in an adult life, regression. I return to my book, which is less compelling, the tension suddenly released. The sun, setting behind their house, darkens the shadow beneath me. They could be anyone, I think. I hear the father say *Not now* and stop what I'm doing.

Intention to Return

In a past life   I was not defined by his death.

. . .   I was not re-routed like a plane through Charlotte.

. . .   I was a part of a "nuclear family," the phrasing
of which appears first in 1924 as "the nuclear family complex."

. . .   I did not have a complex.

. . .   I smiled for the camera.

. . .   Love accumulated like debt—mindless, habit-forming.

. . .   Similes were balanced equations.

. . .   I had my father's face, not "you have your *father's* face."

In a past life   I am on the basketball court behind our apartment
when I hear his footsteps on the asphalt.
(Does it count as a past life if it happened?)

"In a past life"   is not supposed to mean your life before tragedy,
but an existence altogether unrecognizable, which is maybe
the same thing: my having been a fir tree.

In a past life   the stanza above is nonsensical.

In a past life   as a fir tree my identity was also *pine*.

In a past life   that broke off from this one as I watched
a woman walk off of a plane before the doors
were armed, I almost followed her.

In a past life   as that woman, as someone who refused
                      to comply, as a passenger without baggage, without a story
                      she answers to exclusively, no one would know me.

In a past life   the allure is not who we were, but who we are not.

Inertia

In a rented cottage, I fall asleep to the sound of pigeons.
It's hard to picture them above me (on the roof, in the trees?)
and not on the cold ground pulsating quietly in a throng

or pacing the periphery, testing an invisible boundary.
No decision can be made like that, striking at the air, but one
might come to me here in the garden on the brick patio under

the crape myrtle, where days ago I found the hidden key.
My host is home in the main house—she told me I am
welcome there anytime. I think about asking her what I need

to answer for myself. She has a face I've always wanted to grow
into, elegance hardened beyond permeability, but it would turn
back on me, and I'd rather watch her reading in the window.

Further or Farther

In California, my windows are always
open, a kind of porousness I've learned
to accept, that the house across the
street has heard me scream. Outside,

their basset hound is howling. I keep
eating my grapefruit. Each segment is a
day spent the same way, carving its coral
flesh, releasing mist everywhere—juice

rising over the brim like the babbling-
brook effect the neighbors tried to
achieve in their yard. They took a year
to excavate and once the construction

stopped, it rained. The weather used to
govern time. Here, it is a day planner
without dates. When we postponed the
wedding, it felt like getting back a year.

My gym teacher told me to run and
never look back. *You're slowing yourself
down.* I pull apart a split end and follow
it back one year, maybe five? I can hear

my neighbor showing off the water
feature to his guest. Apparently, it is a
swimming pool, but the water against
the river rock looks rank and also cold.

When my mother offered me the side-
stones loose from her engagement ring,
I declined. Said no to her wedding dress
preserved for decades in an acid-free box.

On my desk: their wedding photo in a
box frame, my mother, younger than I
am now, holds a bouquet of lilies
arranged on the bias. They are halfway

down the aisle, my father mid-stride in
a black tuxedo. I tell her I feel farther
away from the life she had at my age.
She says *Further or farther? Do you know*

the difference? Next to the photo, a vase of
strawflowers, the water taking on color,
accumulating silently like a daughter's
rage. Further is figurative, farther is real.

The Concept of Immediacy

I fell asleep with an idea, but when I woke up, I'd lost it,
as when, approaching the rabbit on the trail,
it took off into the brush.
I followed, clearing the warblers,
fixing their gaze.
Ruining something felt like a reason to proceed.
Looking out at the view—
dense swaths of pine, the bay, all three bridges
half-submerged—
I waited for a sign to go back, the mind saying *enough*
or *what next* or *there's nothing here.*
The rabbit had camouflaged itself with the undergrowth.
I wondered if I figured in its sensory system.
Two women came around the bend,
one finishing a sentence: ". . . like, what *I* need."
I had been hearing that a lot lately.
It wasn't what I was thinking,
but related, something about immediacy,
how to experience it.
In the moment of apprehension? Just before?
Or in the lack thereof?
I had a feeling it was the latter.
I would never know when it was happening.

It was time to go. I wanted to stay
and watch the sunset,
the two women still heading up,
but I was afraid to walk down in the dark,
and I wanted to call you and ask you something.

Pendant

You wear him on a necklace—
Saint Christopher carrying a child

across a river. It was your father's
and like any body in motion,

like a pendulum, it would swing
between you and another thing,

which at the start of our relationship
was me. It was always measuring

the distance between us—
how you are Catholic

and I am Jewish, how you thought
your father's sudden death

was not exceptional, but natural.
Whereas I feel my father's death

is the only exceptional thing
I possess.

Till

I was wrong—the day delivered me whole.
You became my husband, that word agrarian,
ill-fitting. Who cared? I was happy
to be a part of expanding time and not outside of it.

After, at a long table, we turned away
from each other briefly to entertain our friends.

I used to worry about the ease
with which you left a room. For years,
I felt closest to love while I was preparing for it—
saying, "I am going to come," so I could.

But I was in unison: My hand; my word. Steadfast.
Remember? The El sped past us in the window.

Summer

Too timid to eat the golden raspberries, I waited until they grew mold
and then hated myself for letting something so beautiful go to waste.
I spent years not letting anyone touch me or look closely at my face or
take my photograph, for I was that certain I would perish under scrutiny.

Today, I find there are berries worth saving, holding one to the light.
In the doorway the only man I am myself with asks what I'm doing.
I am saving the berries from themselves, from forming a constellation.
I am rinsing my hands at the sink, watching soap run through my rings.

Vanitas

When my therapist says grief
ate my adolescence and years
and years after and I ask her

Is it finished? and she says *Is it?*
I picture Cézanne's *Still Life*
with Skull, the mandible

concealed by linen, four pears,
two peaches, and a lemon.
I want to take away the cloth—

to see not what's gold, tart,
sweet, not the decorative fern,
not the worn wood table,

not the ocher wall, not that one
pear pitched like so, unless
it falls and breaks open

on the floor, which is also hidden,
except for a corner, blue,
as if the table were sinking.

I am ready to see the mouth,
the opening, that feasted on time
and left behind this still life.

Sea of Ice

How we forget: *tomb* came from *swell,*
                     swell from the *rise*
     of sea—a *wake*

from an opening in ice.
         A ship—lit by a canopy

of clouds under the cupola
             of night—appears perpetually
in the act of changing course.

           The shrouds lean
into the site of impact—

     breaking light
       into diagonals and planes.

One might fail to notice
    a hull amid the frozen waves.

         Stacked like stones
     they taper to a pinnacle,
simulate a mast.

       Friedrich's painting,
a ship en route to the Arctic,

is en route still

in the parameters of canvas,
                           the coffin of the frame—

the art of wreckage, how to figure ourselves
             in the ruins
                    of what we can't traverse.

An Offering

In art, I was making a teapot
for my mother.
I decided to give it to my teacher.

I had written about my father's
death, and she noted, *lovely.*
After it fired all day in the kiln,

I painted the clay white
with traditional blue flourishes.
Every color had an emotion—

blue was sadness and white too.
Sadness was my method.
Who had taught me that?

I gave her the teapot
on graduation, my teacher
who was everyone's teacher.

Late Interior

based on Before Dinner *by Pierre Bonnard*

Here, the artist has painted a domestic scene
in which two girls, possibly sisters, appear
near a dining table.

One, facing us, stands in front of her plate,
her hands on her lap. The other,
turned away, sits in a yellow chair at the edge
of the frame, where there's likely a fireplace,
its light irradiating the red trim on her robe.

Still, the girls appear in dialogue like the leaves
of a door hinge.

There is no food on the table,
only utensils, a serving tray, a carafe for wine.
A painting on the wall could be from the artist,
known for self-referentiality, drawing attention
to the nature of paint.

The artist creates not from observation
but from memory.

What we're seeing is the overlaying
of many scenes in which two figures cannot
bring themselves to face each other—

the younger girl aligning herself
with the table, the realm of the mother
(not pictured), while the older stays at the hearth,
where their father, who died suddenly,
would normally be.

The skewed perspective allows us to see
the surface of the table and the small dog
underneath waiting for food.

In later interiors, the artist's figures
accrued enough significance
to be freed from their literal shapes, vanishing
altogether from the picture plane.

Imagine harnessing that restraint.

What Is

Hearing you talk to your friend, the sun on your hair,
I thought *she sounds happy*, my mother said.

Happy: like the blue jay settling again on the ponderosa pine.
Look! I said to my mother, and she said, I don't see it,
and then it settled lower.

We were celebrating me—taking crisp walks through woods
and hot soaks in springs. And in between,
the wet walk to the towel, which is what life mostly is.

But I am ungrateful. I was told that again and again
as a child. That I didn't deserve nice things.

I would lie in bed thinking *what is a mother, what is a mother,
what is a mother.*

On the way to the airport she said, I once told your dad
I don't trust nice weather.

I don't either, I said.

She said, try thinking *what is* instead of *what if.*

I came home to rain drilling the gutters and the pipes
and the street and still someone's 80s radio station blared
through the drought-ending symphony.

I couldn't complain. I was drinking wine, watching the lit-up
rain around the streetlamp.

How do I become the streetlamp?

I tell friends, imagine the present is the past
and you will be happier, or imagine the future,
and then think of the present.

Weightless

They're always floating in Chagall—one figure holding another horizontally above a town: Gray gabled roofs. Lone donkey grazing two yards. The boy relieving himself on a fence. The basilica. A round green tree. One fell yesterday on my street and took down a powerline but injured no one. Later, I watched

people gather around to see it on its side. Without rain, the roots had no way to stay attached. I didn't see them haul the trunk away. I went to the beach and watched the seagulls with morsels in their mouths scan the sand for a place to feed. I drove back the other way—one self crossing another self. Sometimes,

I forget which one is real and I ask someone, who tells me, and I disagree and then ask someone else, wanting it to come from above. In *The Promenade*, Chagall with one hand is holding up Bella, flying over him like a pink banner. Looking closer, it could be the weight of her hand against his that keeps her

aloft—her free hand is out of the frame as if she is holding onto something beyond our comprehension. The actual source of her transformation, that love alone cannot provide. I don't know what I thought would bring it about—art, study, self-reflection. I remember all of the balloons I let go, and one in particular, yellow. Watched it go behind a building and then emerge beyond it and then go up higher than I could follow. In *Over Vitebsk*, Bella is pregnant and Chagall's hand, which could also be her hand, is pressed against her belly, as if their child might fall out. She looks worried, stricken, whereas

in *The Birthday*, weeks before they married, she looks surprised, one foot still on the ground, and his body doubled back over hers so that he can kiss her. It's a rare domestic scene, and the town is now out the window, the fences up close. She's holding peonies and eucalyptus and if the painting continued, I could see

her placing them in the vase next to the cake and coin purse on the desk, opening the window and sitting down to write. "I'll stay down here," she'd say, but then I think, no, let her go. I'll stay. Outside, there is no sign of the tree having been there, unless you know to look for it. Soon, someone I know will call,

and I will tell them that it could've fallen on me, if I'd walked the loop that I take most days, repeating the story about what has kept me from some great height and why I always turn right and go up the hill twice, where I can see all of downtown. There's a way to position yourself above where your life is taking place.

Onement

Lifting off
masking tape
from the center
of a freshly
painted canvas,
Barnett Newman
said this
was the beginning
of his life.
Before he'd been
emptying space,
now, filling it.
First, a stripe
of bright red
pigment down
a red brick canvas.
Later, a white line
passing through
cobalt blue.
If the body
were the canvas,
the line
would begin at
the suprasternal
notch,

cross the navel,
and end
between the legs.
I imagine
the space
running through me.
One day,
I will live in it.

Cover the Mirrors

After he died, the mirrors
reflected everything.

The half-face of his friend
walking toward the door,

his wife's back, his sister's
hands. I was there, too,

suspended somewhere
in glass, briefly, indirectly—

What part of me witnessed
myself newly without

my father? I tried not to look.
Cover the mirrors—

Forget yourself to remember the dead.
Someone show me how

to divide the two
when the dead are always here.

When my face is his
conduit. As a girl,

      I sat on my father's sink
      and stared into his mirror

as he shaved his face.
I asked him if it hurt

      as he rounded his chin,
      which was also my chin.

Vanity and grief are closer
than we think.

      Grief's call-and-response
      a mirror of our own making,

an image I can recapture,
walk over to my mother

      and say *look at me, and I*
      will look at you.

Bildungsroman

My father said, do what you love, and the money will follow.
Mrs. Ramsay added, but you'll have to be up with the lark.
My mother said, I had children too early.
We all make our choices, my sister said.
My rabbi said, repeat after me, I am my beloved's
and my beloved is mine.
A crow on the powerline imitated the call of another bird.
My therapist said, tell me what makes you angry.
Canceling our trip, my friend said, I hope you'll understand some day
that it's a decision I need to make.
The lack of moon out my window said the moon
was consorting with the sun.
Acknowledge those who've played a role in your life,
my sign reading said, even if your history is strained,
they have shaped who you are.
My mother said, was it really that bad?
My grandfather after whom I was named said,
when you're on wheels, you're never lost.
Stop trying to figure it out, my handwriting said,
let it reveal itself.
When people cried needlessly my great grandmother was known
to have said, crying with a loaf of bread under their arms.
The obituary said my father said, I'm in a hurry to get well.
I still grieve but I don't dwell on it, my teacher said, there's no point.
My baby brother said, it was harder for you.

Naked before the mirror, my body said, you have not used me enough.
It never feels like the right time, my friend said.
My doctor said, there's plenty of time, I would tell you.
Declare yourself! my grandmother said.

When I Return to Your Room

You are wearing the green robe
I brought with me to college

There's a glass of water
You are drinking it, endlessly

I say, *You must have been thirsty*
You respond by holding up your finger

Can you see the lake
frozen around the perimeter, the snow

dusting the grass?
I touch the window with both hands

as a child does
wanting to be remembered

by the world
When I turn them over,

they are my adult hands
Go outside, you would tell me

The grass is waiting,
the center of the lake is waiting
and still moving

Parentheses

I stream consciousness,
     withhold emotion,
nest inside myself. I shelve

a fleeting thought, manifest
     an echo. I know
your secrets, hear as a hand-

cupped ear. I keep you
     from the point:
I am the life of the poet

(b. 1986, whose life will end
     when I am unified.
Already, I closed around

her father. I was the sound
     of his final word,
a telephone wave, transmitted

to her. I was the hole
     in the ground.
The stone on his grave.

The mourner's yarmulke,
        the mouth
of her grief, the shape

of his face, the cleft
        on his chin, how she
cleaved to him.

The space inside which
        she waits
and waits.

Acknowledgments

Grateful acknowledgment is made to the editors of the journals who first published the following poems (and earlier versions of these poems):

32 Poems: "Prophecy in Blue"; "Mourner's Logic"
The Atlantic: "Invitation"
The Hopkins Review: "Fugue"; "Further or Farther"; "Giverny"; "An Offering"; "Transparent Man"; "When I Return to Your Room"
The Iowa Review: "Diegesis"; "Marrying Houses"
The Kenyon Review: "Mise en Abyme"
New England Review: "Jeanne"; "What Is"
New York Review of Books: "Intention to Return"
Ninth Letter: "Overwinter"
Passages North: "Cocktail Hour"
The Paris Review: "The Concept of Immediacy"; "Echo"; "Narcissus"
Ploughshares: "Cover the Mirrors"
Poetry Northwest: "Parentheses"
A Public Space: "Sea of Ice"
Southern Indiana Review: "Messenger"; "Vanitas"
Tar River Poetry: "The Plans"
The Yale Review: "Caravaggio's *Narcissus*"

Thank you to Jill Bialosky and the entire team at W. W. Norton for believing in this book and making it a reality.

For their professional and artistic support, thank you to the Johns Hopkins Writing Seminars, the University of Southern California, the Stanford University Creative Writing Program, the Bread Loaf Writers' Conference, and the Sewanee Writers' Conference. Thanks especially to my teachers Anna Journey, Sally Keith, Patrick Phillips, Susan McCabe, Mary Jo Salter, Dave Smith, and David Yezzi, as well as Bonnie Seebold and Langdon Hammer for instilling in me a love of poetry. My deepest gratitude to David St. John, and in grateful memory to Louise Glück.

To the incredibly generous readers of these poems—Aria Aber, Shangyang Fang, Amanda Gunn, Alexandria Hall, Richie Hofmann, Jackson Holbert, L. A. Johnson, Elizabeth Metzger, Matt Morton, Catherine Pond, Katherine Robinson, Austen Leah Rose, Melissa Seley, Alison Thumel, Paul Tran, and Keith S. Wilson—thank you for your attention and friendship.

Thank you, Amy, for your insight.

Thank you, Mom, for your life-long support and exemplary way with words; Kate and Will, for your reassurance and encouragement; Michael, for your unwavering belief, humor, and sustaining love; and Faye, for everything.

About the Author

CALLIE SISKEL is the author of *Arctic Revival*, winner of the Poetry Society of America Chapbook Fellowship. Her poems have appeared in *The Atlantic*, *The Paris Review*, and the *New York Review of Books*. A former Wallace Stegner Fellow at Stanford University, she holds a PhD in creative writing and literature from the University of Southern California and lives in Los Angeles.